the **esther** s...
BOOK ONE

I0190953

Meeting
with the
King

Aladeogo-Idaogo Tioluwanimi

SYNCTERFACE
Syncterface Media, London
www.syncterfacemedia.com

MEETING WITH THE KING
Securing a Divine Audience

the **esther** series
BOOK ONE

ISBN: 978-1-912896-18-9

Copyright © June 2024

Aladeogo-Idaogo Tioluwanimi
All Rights Reserved

Published in the United Kingdom by

Syncterface Media, London
www.syncterfacemedia.com
info@syncterfacemedia.com

This book is printed on acid-free paper

Contents

Acknowledgement

To My Heavenly Father,
for keeping your promise to me.

To Jesus, My King,
for revealing Yourself to me most amazingly.

To the Holy Spirit who has been at work in my life
preparing me to meet with the King.

To those who spoke this book forth
by Prophetic Declarations and Prayers.
Thank you for your selflessness.

Desmond Kuku,
for your insightful wisdom, I am grateful.

Chioma, my daughter and precious gift.
Thank you for your words of encouragement
and for insisting on doing the first edit.

Akin Olunloyo, my brother!
Thank you for your selfless kindness
and for sharing your creative gift with me.

Adeola Omisore,
thank you for the gift of editing by the Spirit.

To all who would read this book, I pray that you will
be brought into your personal Meeting with the King.

Prologue

Where did it all begin? As far back as my childhood and teenage years, I remember having this notion that there was a better place beyond the clouds; yes, you could say I spent a lot of time with my head in the clouds. However, somehow, I just could not find the words to capture what I had seen in my mind's eyes.

In my late twenties, when I came to a life of faith through Christ Jesus, I read books written by A.W. Tozer and Madam Guyon, to name a few, who had close relationships with the Lord. This stirred within me a deep yearning to meet Jesus and talk with Him. I wondered what this would be like, but after a while, I thought this was an experience reserved for a select few.

Then came the thought of paradise. I cannot really say when, I first had this thought of paradise. However, I started to see pictures of a place I would describe as out of this world etched upon my imagination. I can only describe it as something beyond words. It was beautiful, simply breathtaking!

While writing, the Holy Spirit reminded me of an experience I had in the year 2014. During worship in a Sunday service, I had an open vision in which I and someone else were led down a path that brought us to the edge of a waterfall; the next thing I knew, we jumped into a place I could only describe as paradise.

Over the years, my hunger for a deeper relationship with Jesus, my Lord, grew. I just always believed there was so much more, and I nurtured this in every way I knew how to (personal time with the Lord, reading books, listening to messages, attending meetings at home and abroad, etc.).

In January 2016, the Lord brought me into a period I called 'One to One'. It was a time of learning to abide in the presence of the Lord, to simply sit at his feet and listen to all He wanted to share with me. There have been other seasons; each helped me grow closer to Him but also brought about a longing for so much more.

In 2018, the Lord summoned me to come before Him as a prelude to what He called 'a defining moment' in my life. On March 26th, 2018, in a vision, I saw a place above the billow of clouds. It had light like the breaking at dawn, an orange-reddish hue, and a song narrative came to me in which I asked the Lord to take me into the reality of what He had shown me:

"Take me beyond the clouds
Take me to the place where You are
For this is paradise, the place of one with You
This is paradise;
there is no other place I would rather be
Take me by the hand and lead me, Lord

Take me to the place where You are
Oh, this is paradise, where all things are made new
This is paradise beauty like I have never seen before
This is paradise, the place of one with you
Take me there."

And this was the Lord's response:

"I will take you by the hand
To the place where I am
For this, I promise you:
I will take you where I am."

While still on this retreat, on the 31st of March 2018, I was shown two paintings that depicted what the Lord had shown me on the 26th, and I thought, Lord, this is truly breathtaking. I was left awestruck by all that had happened.

Looking back, I can see that I did not realise the magnitude of what had happened (thank goodness for the journaling records I had been taught to keep). As the Lord said, He intended to keep His word to me at an appointed time.

The Lord has a specific time when He will accomplish the promises He has made to us.

Promise Fulfilled

In January 2020, I attended "The Secret Place" conference at Revival Fire in Dudley. Before the event, the Holy Spirit had prompted me to go on a personal retreat once I returned from the event. So, on the 26th of January, I set out for my appointment with the Lord. I arrived just after midnight at Ashburnham Place, which, over the years, I have fondly named 'Daddy's House'.

While trying to settle down to sleep, a well-known worship song written by Lenny Le Blanc & Greg Gulley came out of my spirit: "*Down at your feet, oh Lord, is the most high place, In your presence, Lord, I seek your face; I seek your face...*" As I sang this song, a vision opened up to me. I saw a door unlocked and heard 'Access to the King's chamber'. The Lord called my name Aladeogo and said, 'Rest on My bosom; I will show you glorious things in wonder.' This was the beginning of an incredibly intimate season during which the Lord brought me into various encounters with Him. These encounters made God's grandeur, splendour, majesty, and magnificence so real and tangible as He revealed facets of Himself I had not experienced before.

I must have slept off at some point and woke up

to the pitter-patter of rain, and the thought of the scripture that speaks of the sound of the abundance of rain came to me (1 Kings 1:18). This caught my attention as my room number was 118. I thought, "Lord, what is going on here?" I knew He was speaking to me, and I had to pay attention. Next, I heard the Lord say, 'Different time, different place', which He let me understand was a change of season. I spent time reading my bible, seeking to decode what I was being told.

At some point, I came across these verses: "*My eye will see the King in His beauty*" (Isaiah 33:17a). "*In the light of a king's face is life, and his favour is like a cloud of the latter rain.*" (Proverbs 16:15). The encounters were intense, narrative after narrative, drawing me deeper and deeper into different expressions of His Glory. There would never be enough words to express the wave after wave of His Glory. It was truly heaven here on earth; it was real and tangible, and I was like a child who wanted more and more of this endless delight.

Once again, I drifted off to sleep and woke up to the song "Your Majesty" by Muyiwa & Riversongz. While listening, I saw a picture of steps to heaven. Then, the thought of streets paved with gold came to me, and in response to what I was being taken into, I started to say, 'I walk the streets paved with gold.' It was as though I knew I was walking to the throne room of Grace, where the Lord was sitting as King. It seemed like a long walk up the stairs, and at the top, I bowed in reverence, taking off my crown. The King stretched his sceptre to me in approval. As the vision ended, I was given words and a melody as a tale of what had happened, which I titled "**The King has called for me.**"

As I walk the streets paved with gold
I know they lead to the throne of Grace
Before the King of kings, I bow before Him now
Fall on my face and cast down my crown

As my King calls to me
I am awed by His presence
That my King would beckon unto me
To Him, I simply come
Yes, my King, yes, Jesus, yes, my King.
To You, I come

In the presence of Your Majesty,
My heart stops; it skips a beat
That my King calls for me (3ce)
I will dance with my King (3ce)
He has called for me (2ce)

While listening to the song, I heard the Lord say to me, 'I want to take you on a tour of heaven.' Next, I saw these big, thick doors open to a place filled with a brilliant, bright light. Then, a song came to me: **Dance in the Rain of God**.

I will dance in the rain
Till I'm soaked through and through
I will dance in the rain till I'm drenched
I will dance in the rain till it overflows
Till You overflow in me

I will become all You have said
I will become one with the rain
I will dance; I will sing in the rain
I will jump and rejoice in my King (2ce)
Because I know it is bringing
heavenly-born possibilities
I will dance in the rain

The next song was about light: **Take in the glorious light of heaven**.

I take in this light
This glorious light of heaven that I see
It shines so brightly; this glorious light
Let it flood my soul; let it flood my being
That I will see in this light
I will walk in this light
Oh, I take in this light, the light of heaven

I responded by saying
I take in the light of heaven repeatedly
Because You tell me that
in Your light I will see light
Let there be light
Lord, help me see through this light.

I take in this light,
the light of this world,
the light of my life
Lord Jesus, You're my light,
Jesus, You are my light
You shine so brightly and so clearly
Help me see through this light

Then, I was given a revelation from Paul's Road to Damascus conversion found in the book of Acts chapter 9. Now I understand he had to lose the perspective of this world to gain the perspective of Christ.

The messages in songs kept coming one after the other, bubbling forth like a flow of water that just would not stop. They painted, etched, and impressed deep within the reality of the journey of intimacy the Lord was taking me on. I had no idea what surprises He had in store for me. Now, I can also see they were steps taking me to a place designated by the Lord.

On the 28th of January, the Lord continued to woo me into His presence, drawing me closer to where He was. Then I saw a picture of a person by a body of water, and another song, which I called "**By the Water Brook**", came to me.

I will stay with You, Lord; I'll stay
I will sit and wait by the water brook
I'll wait till You come, Lord; I'll wait
I'll wait for You, longing to see Your face
Oh Lord, I wait for You by the water brook

I look into the water and see
a reflection of You in me, Lord
I've become more like You,
One with You, Lord,
I see Your face looking back at me
as I look into the water brook

I was brought into a moment of asking the Lord to take all my heart, which brought me another narrative: **Let us meet in the deep**.

While listening to this narrative, I heard the Lord say to give Him undivided attention over the next three days. As I pondered over all that had happened so far, it stood out that the Lord said He would give me a tour of heaven. As I went through my notes over the last few days, I felt the need to read the Book of Revelation 21:1: "*..I saw a new heaven and a new earth for the first heaven and the first earth had passed away.*" I thought, hmm, Lord, what does this mean? Things are not as before; all things are made new.

On the 29th of January, as this journey continued to unfold, the day started with the Holy Spirit raining down on us from above. The walk led me into the 'Garden of the Lord', where the Lord had more things to share with me. Next was an invitation to stop by the 'Well of the Lord' and drink from the well of life (there was an actual well to sit by). After a while, as I continued my walk, I picked up this lovely scent, and as I tried to find its origin, another song came to me:

I smell a fragrance drawing me
I smell this beautiful fragrance drawing me
I smell this fragrance drawing me
I smell this beautiful fragrance drawing me

Lord, I smell the fragrance of my King

Lord, I smell Your fragrance drawing me
I smell the fragrance of the Lord drawing me

I see Your beauty in the buds
that are breaking forth
But above all,
I smell the fragrance of the Lord drawing me

(As I close my eyes to recall the experience again, I hear my heart say, Lord, I miss you dearly)

Also, in the same space, I became so conscious of the sun shining in the sky. It was as though the Lord was smiling down on me. Another torrent of melody overflowed in my heart; it caused joy and delight to bubble up in me, and I found myself laughing like a child being tickled by her father. I was responding to what was going on. It was not a figment of my imagination. It was so real to me; it filled me with awe, simply a wonder to behold. The presence of the Lord was intensely tangible, and that's when He brought the conversation about Esther to me. While trying to take in all that was happening, gently and clearly, I heard the Lord say to me, "You know this is a book, right, "Meeting with The King."

2

How to Meet with the King

As I pondered the question, 'How do you meet with a king?' I heard the word Preparation. Preparation is key when it comes to meeting with the King.' Then, while musing, 'How do you prepare to meet with a king?' I heard, 'There is an outward preparation and, more importantly, an inward preparation of the heart.

The Outward Preparation

I want us to imagine receiving an invitation to meet with the Queen of England (*When I first wrote this, the Queen was still alive, but now King Charles sits on the throne. I might be inclined to take that as a prophetic sign, considering the title of the book*). This would immediately throw you into a process of preparation. What do I wear to this event of a lifetime? The answer is simply, "Only the best would do", and then, the mission to go shopping to find the best dress, accessories, handbags, shoes, etc. or even have something designed specifically for this grand occasion would begin. The thought of what the day would look like would fill one's mind, and the list of questions you would ask yourself would go on and on.

So, this brings us to the crux of the matter: What do we wear to meet the King of all Kings? The setting of 'Meeting with the King', as the Lord showed me, is found in one of my favourite books in the Bible, the book of Esther.

Long ago, Esther received a summons to meet the King. While she was living her normal life in Shushan with her uncle Mordecai, who adopted her after the death of her parents, she was unaware major events were unfolding in the palace that was about to disrupt and change the course of her life forever. In the palace, King Ahasuerus was having a banquet, during which he called for his queen Vashti, but Vashti refused to answer her king's call. Do we know it is possible to decline the invitation to meet with the King? My heart shuddered when I thought about this. Yet the King called for Vashti so he could show off her beauty (Esther 1:11).

How unfortunate for Vashti. Why did Vashti refuse the king? At that moment, she felt her business was more important than the King's; after all, she, too, had made a feast for the women in the palace (Esther 1:9). She had a big lapse in judgment; she was queen in the first place because the King had chosen her. I hear you say, 'How does this apply to us?' When the King of Kings calls for us, do we remember that we are royalty because He chose us, or, like Queen Vashti, are we too busy doing 'our own thing', doing what we think is important, thus neglecting the call of the King and the things that are important to Him?

Vashti's misconduct also had far-reaching consequences; it reflected badly on the King, making it look like he had no honour in His house, and his queen was a bad example to women throughout the Kingdom (Esther 1:17-18). Vashti's response to the King cost her position as queen and eventually led to her being banished from the palace altogether (Esther 1:19). She fell from a place of much grace to the grass, as the expression goes. We have much to learn from Vashti's mistakes, and it is the desire to live out our idea of what we think or believe our lives should be, ignoring God's purpose, which is our unsurpassed life.

Let us think about this for a moment: Are there areas where the Lord is calling our attention to relinquish our hold or personal agenda so that we can come to His best thoughts and work out His plan for our lives?

The Inward Preparation of the Heart

Esther's introduction to us starts with the chronicle of seemingly unfortunate life circumstances that brought her to live with her uncle Mordecai in Shushan (Esther 2:5-7). Then we are told about her physical beauty, *".... The young woman was lovely and beautiful"*. When she is taken into the palace with the many others whose lives were also overtaken unexpectedly, she stands out in both conduct and character. How? Well, Esther was found to be pleasing to Hegai, the custodian of the women (Esther 2:9). I deduce that Esther must have behaved in a manner that stood out from the others; she did not let being in the palace go to her head. There is a maxim that says, 'Attitude leads to altitude.' Being well-behaved leaves a lasting impression. Unlike Vashti, Esther was not presumptuous about the situation at hand and was patient enough to let things unfold. Esther's fortitude should be noted. We will see how this holds her in good stead later on.

The Bible tells us of Esther's journey into the palace. First, the royal decree went out in the land, which summoned and gathered all the beautiful young virgins. (Esther 2:2-3). The call went out to all, and there would also be a selection process for the one who would be crowned Queen. The verse Matthew 22:14 springs to mind, "*For many are called, but few are chosen.*" Decisive choices should not be handled lightly or carelessly during the transition between being called and being chosen.

Also, your response is crucial in going from being called to being chosen. The palace was a new territory that Esther had to adapt to quickly. Her ability to embrace and adjust to the new was crucial. While at home with her uncle Mordecai, Esther developed the ability to receive proper guidance. We deduce from this that what the Lord has taught us during one season will help us in the next season, which will open us up to His new or next place for us.

Being in the palace does not mean you are before

the King. Esther had to embark on a twelve-month preparatory journey to meet the King. The Bible tells us, *"Each young woman's turn came to go into King Ahasuerus after she had completed twelve months' preparation, according to the regulations for the women, for thus were the days of their preparation apportioned"* (Esther 2.12). The first time I read this, and even now, I was filled with wonder. I mean, why did it take twelve months to prepare? For the first six months, the young women were treated with oil of myrrh. What is the oil of myrrh? Then, for the second six months it was perfumes and cosmetics.

For you and me, the first six with the oil of myrrh is our process of dying to our selfish ways; this means giving up what we have planned for our life in its entirety. However, there is no quick fix for this, and the Lord patiently works on us. What I want to highlight is that preparation is a thorough process. The six months of perfumes and cosmetics, in our case, is the process by which our lives become a sweet-smelling aroma to the Lord.

The scripture that was a mantra for a particular season in my life is found in the book of Romans:

> [1] *I appeal to you therefore, brethren, and beg of you in view of (all) the mercies of God, to make a decisive dedication of your bodies (presenting all your members and faculties) as a living sacrifice, holy (devoted, consecrated), and well pleasing to God, which is your reasonable (rational, intelligent) service and spiritual worship."*
>
> **~ Romans 12:1 AMPC**

When we have offered our lives as a living sacrifice

with the foremost desire to please and live for the Lord our God, the fragrance of Christ is diffused through our lives and draws others to Him.

Palace Protocol and Etiquette

One day, I heard the Lord say to me, 'You need to learn the protocol of the palace'. Once inside, Esther learned the decorum of the palace by submitting to the tutelage of the one who was best acquainted with the King.

> [8] *So it was, when the king's command and decree were heard, and when many young women were gathered at Shushan the citadel, under the custody of Hegai, that Esther was also taken to the King's palace, into the care of Hegai, the custodian of the women.* [9] *Now, the young woman pleased him, and she obtained his favour. So, he readily gave her beauty preparations besides her allowance. Then seven choice maidservants were provided for her from the king's palace, and he moved her and her maidservants to the best place in the house of the women.*
> ~ *Esther 2:8-9 NKJV*

I believe Esther demonstrated that she had the ability to receive and be taught what she did not know.

In being invited to meet with the King, one must learn the protocols and etiquette of Palace life, such as, How do I behave in the palace? What must I do to please the King? etc. As we see from the account of events, being in the Palace is only the first phase of "Meeting with the King."

In Esther Chapter 2, the Holy Spirit drew my attention to the fact that Esther's first port of call was the house of women. Here, how she related with others would show her entrenched allure. Learning to relate with others is central to our journey to meet the King. We would evolve through the shaping of our character in how we relate with others in all kinds of circumstances, be it those who love us or those who do not, for whatever reason.

What the Lord progressively works out in us is being Christ-like. We are shaped through relational challenges with family, friends, and acquittances, which, in God's hand, ultimately grow our love walk, which starts with God and extends to those around us. I would be the first to say it is easier said than done; however, this passage of rite is inevitable. The Lord has given us all the help we need, as found in the book of Philippians:

> [13] *(Not in your own strength) for it is God Who is all the while effectually at work in you (energising and creating in you the power and desire), both to will and to work for His good pleasure and satisfaction and delight.*
> ~ ***Philippians 2:13 AMPC***

It is reassuring to know God is always our very present help in every situation.

Esther and the other young women knew the King would only choose one of them as queen. Imagine how this would have impacted on them. We can infer that when her uncle Mordecai kept watch over her, he also continued to counsel her on how to conduct herself and that Esther listened. For you and me, the amazing Holy Spirit is the voice of counsel and the one assigned to teach us about our King.

I am reminded of what Jesus said, "When the Holy Spirit comes, He will teach us all things. May I ask how attentive we are to the one who knows our King the best? The Holy Spirit is the most important person we can walk with on the face of the earth and this side of eternity. Why? I hear you ask. Because He knows the mind of God concerning you and me. As we continue in fellowship and building a relationship with Him, He longs to share and make much known to us. When we think of meeting the King, do we yield to the Holy Spirit to work in us to make us fit and ready to meet our King? The fruit of the Spirit is His work of beautifying us.

> *11 So the King will greatly desire your beauty;*
> *Because He is your Lord, worship Him.*
> *13 The royal daughter is all glorious within the palace;*
> *Her clothing is woven with gold.*
> *14 She shall be brought to the King in robes of many colors;*
> *The virgins, her companions who follow her, shall be brought to You.*
> *~ Psalm 45:11,13,14 NKJV*

At the beginning of 2020, these verses helped me so much when the Lord introduced Himself to me as King and spoke to me about colours and royalty. Let us take some time to ponder these words deeply.

4

Pleasing the King

During the time of preparation, Esther and the others would have been instructed in what I call 'Pleasing the King'. Why? So there would not be a repeat of what happened to the former queen, Vashti. Therefore, training the incoming queen candidates would have become critical and central.

To please the King is to have His utmost interest at heart. You see, becoming the new queen hinged on this. Yet, I wonder how many of them paid attention and sought to find out what would be pleasing to the King. Did these women seek to make the King the object of their affections, or did they allow themselves to be distracted by the opulence of the palace and its lifestyle, forgetting why they were there in the first place? Again, my attention was drawn to the fact that each woman was given what she desired to take from the women's quarters to the king's palace, and in that moment, I thought, did some of the women settle for that, as all there is?

The Holy Spirit revealed to me that Esther was paying close attention; you might ask, how do I know that? The Bible tells us.

15 Now when the turn for Esther the daughter of Abihail, the uncle of Mordecai who had taken her as his own daughter, had come to go in to the king, she required nothing but what Hegai the king's attendant, the keeper of the women, suggested. And Esther won favor in the sight of all who saw her.

~ *Esther 2:15 AMPC*

Esther listened to the one who knew the King best. Are we listening to the One who knows the King best? Have we cultivated a relationship with the Holy Spirit to obtain His favour so He might take you and me to meet with the King? Do we know the person of the Holy Spirit delights in introducing us to the King and helping us to grow closer and more intimate with the One called the Lover of our soul?

Another important thing to note is that unless the King delighted in her to call for her again by name, each woman only had one chance to meet the King. Only one visit, and if you were not chosen, it was over! Let us ponder on this: Does our King know us by name to call for us again and again? We should desire that He would come and dwell with us. So, just imagine, each woman was called in for their night with the King, and one by one, they were rejected. I am curious to know what transpired that left the King unsatisfied with each one of them until Esther came along.

As we read slowly and contemplatively, let us stand in these women's shoes, try to comprehend what the Lord might want us to see and make the necessary adjustments where possible.

I came across the song **'One Night With the King'**

by Jonathan Butler and Juanita Bynum. The message in this song paints a beautiful picture.

One night with The King
Changes everything
One day in His courts
Did forever change my course
One moment in His presence
And I've never been the same
One night with the King
Changes everything

One night with the King
Changes everything
One day in His courts
Could forever change your course
One moment in His presence
And you'll never be the same
One night with the King
It changes everything

From the desert to the King
It had been my destiny
To be chosen for such a time as this
I didn't know that all of my dreams
Could become realities
Then I saw His face
His love captured me

Yes, one night with the King
Oh, it really changes everything
Just one day in His courts
It will forever change your course

All you need tonight is just
One moment in His presence
Just one moment in His presence
Hey, oh, one moment in His presence
And you'll never be the same

One night with the King
It changes (everything)
One day in His courts
It changes (everything)
One night with the King
It changes everything

I know that it changes
It changes everything
Yes it does

When preparing to meet with the King we should be determined to come into His presence with our very best. Let these words and imagery reshape how we come to the King of our lives. Have we learned to make Him the sole object of our affection? I ask that we stop and think about this for a moment as we continue on our personal journey to meeting the King of Kings. Asking yourself the following questions might help:

- How do I please the King?
- Is my life pleasing to the King, my God, and my King?
- Am I living for Him and Him only?

"Have we cultivated a relationship with the Holy Spirit to obtain His favour so He might take you and me to meet with the King?"

The Greatest Love of All

The story of Esther and the King serves as a backdrop for us to appreciate and seek the love of our King, the greatest love of all. To win the heart of the King, it must be our priority; our heart carriage before him must be ardent affection. While reading the book of Esther, this verse caught my attention:

> [17] the king loved Esther more than all the women, and she won grace and favor in his sight more than all the virgins, so that he set the royal crown[a] on her head and made her queen instead of Vashti.
>
> ~ *Esther 2:17 ESV*

Esther's story can also be viewed through the lenses of 'love lost' and 'love recovered'. It reminds me of our salvation story; our fellowship and love relationship with God were lost in the garden but restored through Christ Jesus. Love underpins everything God does. It is the unending theme in the Bible from Genesis to Revelation: God's love for the world He created.

The book of the Songs of Songs is an allegory of our love relationship with God. The poetic language used depicts the depth of intimacy between two lovers, the King and the Shulamite woman. Reading

The Song of Songs helped realign my heart's love dynamics with the King. Let it captivate you and me, as we are called to be lovers of God and Jesus, our King. God is love, and as we encounter God, His love invades our hearts, and we ultimately become love.

Our heart posture is to affectionately pursue the King. A song titled; "**King of My Heart**" by Steffany Gretzinger comes to mind. It tells a story of God being good, dependable and reliable in every way. On my journey to meet with the King, I remember having to give all my heart to Him.

Let us think about how we come to our heavenly King as we come to Him. Does God look forward to seeing us when we turn up? Can God call you "A man after My heart," like King David?

As we read King David's writings in the Psalms, it is clear that God had first place in his heart and life. One of my favourites is Psalm 51, which shows the remorse in David's heart when he finally realised the enormity of what he had done wrong. The distinctiveness of his relationship with God made King David one of the most unforgettable characters in the Bible.

Queen Esther was beautiful. We are told that she looked stunning. Esther also exhibited inner strength, which she displayed at different stages of her journey. The trait that would have endeared her to the King was the inward beauty of the heart. I believe that is why she won the King's heart out of the many. Once she became Queen, she demonstrated that she had the King's interest at heart. She approached him with the utmost reverence, esteem, and honour when she wanted to speak to the King.

As I thought about what these words mean regarding how we approach our King, the first thing that came to mind was that reverence is synonymous with worship. We were created to worship, so we must posture ourselves in worship before our King. Worship is simply us recognising and ascribing the worth of our God and King in our lives in everything we do. Esteem and honour presage the recognition of who our King is.

The greatest honour we can give Him is the utmost place in our lives. When Queen Esther had to come before the King with a pressing matter, she handled the delicate issue with sensitive wisdom. In that moment, we see Esther standing before God to do His will and yet being able to hold with delicate balance the heart of a man, King Ahasuerus. As women, we can learn from and apply this to our relationships with God and man.

Without a shadow of a doubt, pleasing God was paramount in her heart. Queen Esther was a person of inner strength. we see her resolve come forth when it was most needed in her statement, *"If I perish, I perish..."* (Esther 4:16). She had made her mind up to lay her life on the line to accomplish the task of saving her people from pending annihilation. She won the battle by using the divine strategy not to reveal her identity as a Jew until the appointed time.

6

Who is the King?

I want to introduce us to the King. His name is King Jesus. How do I know He is King? David the King opened up an eternal portal for us to look through when he said, "*The LORD said unto my Lord, sit at my right hand...*" (Psalms.110:1a).

Daniel, by vision, took us into the throne room of the Ancient of Days. There, we are told that of His Kingdom, there shall be no end. The kingdoms of this world have become the Kingdom of our God. In the book of Revelation, we are taken into the Throne Room of Heaven and shown Christ Jesus as the one who sat on the throne.

> ¹⁶ *And He has on His robe and on His thigh a name written: KING OF KINGS AND LORD OF LORDS.*
> ~ ***Revelation 19:16 NKJV***

The metaphors of the Psalms, Isaiah, Daniel's vision, and the Revelations of John portray and help us fully comprehend that Jesus Christ is the King. What a privilege that we have been invited to meet the King! The accounts of Esther and King Ahasuerus are parallels from which we can draw.

The Reason for the Invitation

May I let you in on a secret? The invitation to meet with the King is a progression into an intimate relationship with Him. Jesus came to restore our broken communion with God. Why? Because without it, we have no life; we were not created to exist independently of God. Intimacy with the King would subsequently bring us into the purpose and destiny earmarked for us. In the budding of this love relationship, we are drawn closer to our King.

Meeting Place with The King

In March 2020, while in Windsor, I had a very strong impression of visiting the palace. One of the rooms I passed through was the King's chambers, and it struck me that it was built for intimacy.

In the backdrop story, we see that the meeting place of Esther and the King is alone in his chambers. This is where we learn to give our King undivided attention and prioritise our relationship with Him. Reading about the King and Esther, a statement that caught my attention was: *"And the king loved Esther more than all the women,…"* (Esther 2:17).

The first time or place we met our King Jesus

was through His demonstration of our Heavenly Father's love towards us:

> [16] For God so loved the world that He gave His only begotten Son, that whoever believes in Him should not perish but have everlasting life.
>
> ~ *John 3:16 NKJV*

The King wants to take you and me on an eternal adventure that starts here and ends in heaven. In the framework of Queen Esther's story, she brought something that made her irresistible to the King. Therefore, I ask, "Are we making ourselves alluring to our King? The scripture says:

> [1] Beautiful words fill my mind as I compose this song for the King. Like the pen of a good writer, my tongue is ready with a poem.
>
> ~ *Psalm 45:1 GNT*

What do you say to the King? Do you let Him know how much you love and adore Him? Is your voice and heart distinct out of the many? Is the King the object of your desire?

When Queen Esther met with the Heavenly King, it prepared her for the purpose He had for her. You might ask, what is the purpose? Through her, a people were saved, and the knowledge of God was also revealed to a people who did not previously know the God of the Israelites.

"...reverence is synonymous with worship.
We were created to worship, so we must posture ourselves in
worship before our King"

The Beginning, not the end

This is merely an introduction to all that awaits us as we journey along the path to meeting with the King of Kings, Jesus. While the King asked me to write this, my season of Meeting the King has not ended; it is still ongoing. I long for more of Him. What about you?

If reading this has stirred your heart to seek our King more than ever, I believe my work is done. It is not the end but the beginning of the endless possibilities of meeting with the King.

A Prayer

Heavenly Father, I thank You for the invitation to each one who reads the words of this book to be brought into their own season/place of Meeting with You, The King. Let them experience the fullness of what John the Revelator wrote, "And I heard a loud voice from heaven saying "Behold the tabernacle of God is with men and He will dwell with them, and they shall His people, and He shall be their God *(Revelation 21:3)*, in Jesus' name. Amen

www.ingramcontent.com/pod-product-compliance
Lightning Source LLC
Chambersburg PA
CBHW051242020426
42331CB00017B/3487